DAR 6-8-18

To: Bette
and I,

God Bless You,

T. C Christman

Marie Michell Robinson:
A Soaring Pioneer

T.C. Christman

Sterling
Book Press

Sterling Book Press
7007 Metro Pkwy #321
Sterling Heights, MI 48311
Website: www.sterlingbookpress.com
Email: sterlingbookpress@gmail.com

First published by Sterling Book Press in December 2017

ISBN: 978-0-9996030-0-0

Library of Congress Control Number: 2017961428

Printed in the United States of America

This book is printed on acid-free paper.

Because of the dynamic nature of the Internet, any website addresses or links contained in this book may have changed since publication and may no longer be valid.

TABLE OF CONTENTS

ACKNOWLEDGEMENTS

I would like to thank Wanda Langley, Tom and Sheri Roose, Joe Hansen, the Project Remembrance Team, Roy Michell, my daughter Cheryl Marie Michell, and my beloved husband James Christman.

I have been crucified with Christ and I no longer live, but Christ lives in me. The life I now live in the body, I live by faith in the Son of God, who loved me and gave himself for me.

— Galatians 2:20

CHAPTER 1

Growing Up

World War I had just ended, the Victorian and Edwardian eras were over, and the famous "Roaring Twenties" had just entered the social world of America. Following the recent war, airplanes were more popular and commercial radio programming was a growing new medium. Women were cutting their long hair and shortening their skirts. Men were shaving their beards and wearing spats (a simple covering over their shoes to keep them polished). Many societal changes were taking place as well, and women were eager to take advantage of the times. They wanted to vote and were opening their own businesses.

Marie's story is awe-inspiring. It started when she was born in Detroit, Michigan, on May 23, 1924, to Roy and Ruth Michell, just sixteen months after her brother, Roy Jr., had been born on January 12, 1923. Marie had a special charisma about her even as a young girl. To Roy, however, she was at times a pest. Since they were so close in age they often acted like twins. In fact, their mother would refer to them as "Tate and Imitate." Marie was forever trying to outdo her brother Roy, whom she adored. Since Roy was reading when he started kindergarten, Marie made sure she was reading before kindergarten, too.

While Roy and Marie were impressionable young kids, Charles Lindbergh made aviation history in 1927 by flying solo across the Atlantic Ocean to Europe. Amelia Earhart was making news and growing in popularity, too, as she became a celebrity for her flying skills and promoting aviation wherever she went.

The excitement of the Roaring Twenties ended with a sudden crash in 1929, though, and the Great Depression set in. The stock market fell to the floor and all of America was in shock. Men were jumping out of buildings and shooting themselves because they were now paupers instead of millionaires. And in 1931 Marie and Roy Jr.'s parents got a divorce, which was unheard of in those days.

Mrs. Ruth Michell took her two young children back to Michigan to see her own mother, Kate Jackson, and her sister, Flo Krall. She needed to try to pull herself and her little family together, trying hard to make sense out of all the chaos going on in the world. It was good to talk with her sister who had been her partner in their hat design business in the Fisher Building in Detroit.

Grandma Kate would babysit the children when Ruth was busy. Marie loved her grandmother and all her stories about their relative Stonewall Jackson. Grandma Kate's husband, Henry John Jackson, was the son of Isaac Jackson, a second cousin of Stonewall. Isaac and Stonewall had the same great-grandfather, John Jackson, who was born in Ireland around 1716, immigrated to the United States, and died in 1801 in Clarksburg, West Virginia. On the genealogy tree, Marie was the seventh generation of the Jackson family in America; her mother Ruth, the sixth; Grandpa Henry John, the fifth; Isaac, the fourth; Henry J., the third; another Henry, the second; and John, the first.

Marie was so vivacious and happy that Grandma Kate would often admonish her to slow down and smell the roses. They loved each other dearly and enjoyed teasing each other.

After a while Ruth met a new friend named Major Maurice Zetterholm, known to his friends as "Zet". He married Ruth in 1932, and now her two children had a new stepfather who was in the army and travelled a lot.

For his seventh and eighth grades, Roy was enrolled in Morgan Park Military Academy near Chicago. At the same time, Marie was enrolled in Dorothy Dorben's School of Dance. Marie was a "natural" and began to excel in ballet dancing. As a teenager she even was allowed to dance at the Edgewater Beach Hotel with the professional Dorothy Dorben Dancers, which was quite a privilege.

In 1936, Roy went to St. John's Military Academy in Delefield, Wisconsin, and met Jack Hayward. Roy and Jack were the "new boys," and hazing of various degrees was the norm for newcomers. Most of the "old boys" did it in good nature, but there were some who delighted in

Marie Michell, at about eight years old, smelling the roses with her Grandma Kate (Norris) Jackson. Grandma Kate's husband, Henry John Jackson, was the son of Isaac Jackson, a second cousin of Stonewall Jackson. Painting by T.C. Christman.

carrying it to extremes. At any rate, Jack soon left the academy but would return his junior year.

During his time away, Jack had taken bodybuilding and judo courses; it was evident that anyone who felt like hazing him in any manner would be taking his life into his own hands. Jack and Roy quickly became good friends. After Jack had a chance to meet Roy's adorable sister, Marie, they became even closer friends. Marie fell in love with Jack, and that was all she could talk about. She was sixteen years old now and was going to an all-girls school in Maryland called National Park Junior College. She kept begging her mother to make her a hat and dress her up for Roy's graduation ceremony in the spring of 1940. The school took a picture of Jack and Roy with Marie in the middle, wearing her new hat.

Roy attended Northwestern University in 1940 and was planning on enlisting rather than being drafted. That way he could select what branch of service he would be in. He ultimately decided to attend the University of Arizona for one full year and then enlist in the Naval Air Training at Wooster College in Ohio. He was sent back to Detroit in 1942 with the Dean of Highland Park Junior College, which sponsored a Naval Flight training class at Masonic Airport near Selfridge Field on the grounds of the old Masonic Country Club.

Meanwhile, Marie was so eager to grow up. She had a bubbly personality and was fun to be around, as young as she was and with a sweet nature and those beautiful light green eyes. When they were younger, she and her brother used to look into each others eyes to see who had the greenest eyes. Roy felt he won because his eyes were darker, whereas hers were a light green. Grandma Kate continued to remind her to slow down and smell the roses because she would be grown up for a long time; now, however, she should enjoy her youth.

Marie learned all about Jack taking flying lessons when he was sixteen years old and how much he loved it. She was so awestruck with Jack that his ability to fly was all she would talk about. Now she had to learn to fly, too. She had two more years before she was to graduate in 1942, so she began to take flying lessons without her family knowing about it. She secretly took flying lessons with her roommate, Carolyn Viers Mudgett, who had a car and would drive them to their lessons at Congressional Airport. Coincidentally, both of their instructors were named "Mac".

Jack Hayward, Marie Michell and Roy Michell Jr. at Roy's graduation ceremony in 1940. Marie, 16 years old, is wearing the new hat her mother made for her especially for the occasion.

As a surprise to Marie's father on his birthday, October 1, 1942, she took him to the airport and flew solo for him after she had graduated from high school and pilot's school. Later he would often tell others how she scared him spitless!

After Marie graduated in June of 1942, she attended Vanderbilt University in Tennessee for a brief time. Vanderbilt was a co-ed school, and there she became reacquainted with Gray Stahlman, a friend of her brother who had graduated from St. John's Military Academy a year prior to Roy and was now attending Vanderbilt University as well. Since Marie previously had gone only to all-girls schools, this was an opportunity to meet a few more boys.

The Webster's Dictionary that Marie had received when she enrolled at Vanderbilt University provides interesting clues to her social life during this time. On one of the back empty pages she had written two names: Jack Hayward on top and C.A. McKay below. A third name was mostly erased but still readable. First it said, "*and also maybe Gray Stahlman,*" possibly written by Gray himself. Across the last page in the dictionary was written in Gray's handwriting in very bold words: "*Forget I ever existed*" with a line through it, then "*Love ya' . . . Me.*" Then some more erased words: "*Notice . . . (?) . . . Marie you're an angel . . . (?) . . .*" And on the previous page Gray had written in bold letters: "*Marie Darlin: Love you more than anything in the world always will. Dream up a couple.*" It was signed: "*All My Love . . . Gray*".

Marie's brother Roy felt that Gray's mother did not care for Marie. Maybe it was that she was a student of Dorothy Dorben's School of Dance and was dancing at the Edgewater Beach Hotel with the Dorben Dancers and perhaps met Gray there. Or maybe it was because of her love for flying. Who knows? But Marie did not feel comfortable with Gray and soon broke off her interest in him.

CHAPTER 2

At Avenger Field and Meeting Kit

After graduating from high school in 1942, Marie became a "Link Trainer" instructor, using the flight simulation machine to teach students how to fly by instruments. She did this from June of 1942 until September of 1943. She also was still corresponding with Jack as much as she could and constantly told her friend Carolyn how much she wanted to impress Jack. After all, Jack's father, mother and sister were all pilots.

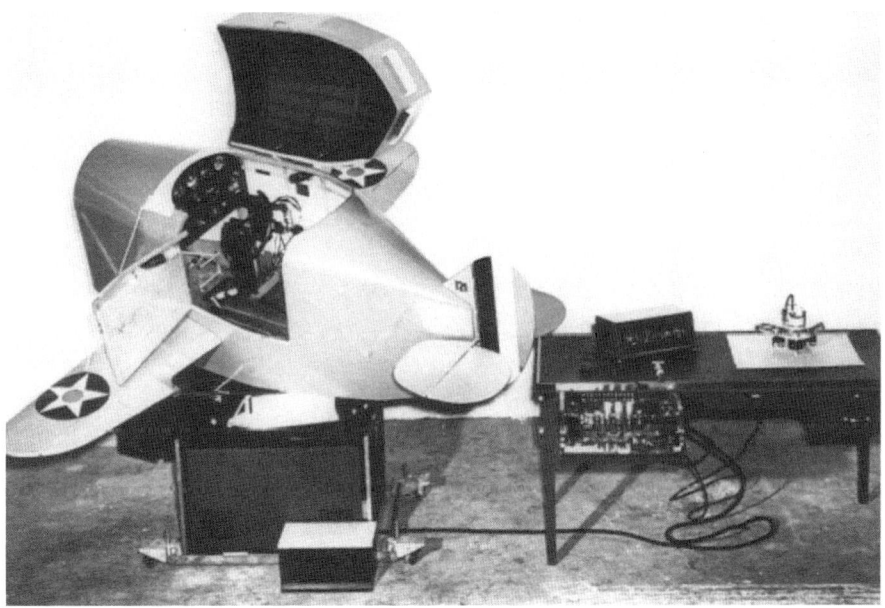

The Link Trainer was invented by David Link in 1929. As a flight simulator that responded to the pilot's controls and determined how well the trainee performed, it was a key teaching aid for thousands of new pilots during WWII.

America was at war now. When the Japanese attacked Pearl Harbor on December 7, 1941, everyone instantly became serious American patriots. Even high school seniors were no longer kids. They were going to end that war in a hurry after they graduated.

Things had changed tremendously in America because of the war. Everything went first to the government. Items had to be rationed. People needed permits to buy anything, including gas for their cars. There were even rations on how much meat people could buy. To get around this restriction, some people would go to Canada every so often, buy meat there, and would then wear it home because, although they could purchase all they wanted in Canada, they were technically not allowed to bring it back over the border.

No new cars were being built due to the government requiring auto manufacturers to build tanks and air planes and bombs, etc. Car owners would get retreads on their tires, which resulted in highways strewn with chunks of retread rubber from flat retread tires. All metal was used for the war, and children were encouraged to give their metal toys to the government so the metal could be used for the war efforts. As often as they could, children also paid 25 cents for war bond stamps, which eventually would fill up a stamp book and be cashed in after the war.

It was a different time back then. No new golf balls were produced; golfers used old smiley-faced golf balls instead. Plastic, though invented, was not a common commodity. Kleenex was not created yet, so everyone carried hankies. Women never wore slacks, only dresses. During the summer, though, they did wear long shorts called culottes. The most popular shoe style of the time was the saddle shoe, which was a white oxford shoe with a piece of brown or black leather stitched across the instep. They were the rage. Marie wore them with her flying clothes, as seen in several pictures and paintings of her.

Frozen food was unheard of then; the only item kept frozen at home was ice cubes, and in Detroit, people were still getting ice for their icebox via a horse-drawn cart. Grocery stores were small mom and pop shops. The milkman delivered eggs, milk, cream and butter every day.

Homes did not have television sets at this time. Instead, people gathered around to listen to the radio. One of the most popular programs in the country was that of Father Charles E. Coughlin, the pastor of Royal Oak's Shrine of the Little Flower Catholic Church. He spoke on political and financial issues and social justice. He warned against communism coming from Russia and the evil teachings of socialism. He questioned and had a difficult time understanding why the Jews would give up the God of Abraham, Isaac and Jacob to become atheists. Millions of people across the nation listened to Father Coughlin's broadcasts.

The country was very much united in its war efforts. The newscasts did not include opinion and commentary against the government's position. There was no great dissension when German and Japanese people in the United States were put in detention centers during the war. Also noteworthy, the Holocaust of the Jewish people in Europe was not really known or publicized.

Marie moved to Sweetwater, Texas, on Sept 6, 1943, boarding the military bus to Avenger Field, which was the largest all-women training center in American history. She had heard all about Jacqueline Cochran and the Women Airforce Service Pilots (WASP) organization starting up to help America end World War II. Marie wanted to join these brave pioneers and serve her country the best way she could as a productive pilot in the war. There were only 1,830 candidates selected for the program from a field of 25,000 applicants, and each felt honored and privileged for the opportunity. Only 1,074 graduated. Out of eighteen classes, Marie's group was the tenth class overall, known as 44-W-2, the second class to graduate in 1944.

The greatest tragedy that Marie would ever experience in her young life was soon to occur. She was not used to all the changes in living conditions, but camp life had taught her "to rough it!" So for her country she would.

Those who knew Marie saw her as a fun-loving little gal who lit up the room when she walked into it. She had a hard time sitting still because she loved to dance and would do her ballet steps every now and then. She was very gracious and did not want to antagonize anyone. She wanted them as her friends.

It was during this time that Marie met Elizabeth MacKethan, or "Kit," as she was called. Kit would become her closest friend for the rest of her brief life. She was six years older than Marie, which Marie was glad about since it was her secret dream to have an older sister who would help guide her on a lot of decisions that parents didn't really understand because they were so much older. Kit told Marie all about her experiences in North Carolina, how she had graduated from college, when she had learned to fly and teach instrument flying using the Link Trainer, the same as Marie. It was so good for Marie to meet someone she could relate to and share dreams together.

Jacqueline Cochran established the Women Airforce Service Pilots (WASP) organization in 1943. She was well known for her flying abilities, having set numerous records in her career. "Jackie" was the first woman to fly a bomber across the Atlantic, and on May 18, 1953, became the first woman to break the sound barrier.

Marie told Kit about her fiancé, Jack Hayward, and how he had been in military school with her brother Roy for so many years and had enlisted in the Navy as a pilot. She explained that she had taken up flying because of Jack, and now she and Jack were planning on getting married after the war was over.

Usually when people meet someone new in their life they share only sweet things like happy moments, but Marie felt so comfortable with Kit that she started sharing the struggles, difficulties and confusing parts of her life. She talked about how as a kid her folks were divorced and she was no longer able to see her dad easily. When her mother remarried, they moved more often because Marie's stepfather was a Major in the U.S. Army. They started in Birmingham, Michigan; went to Larchmont, New York; then New Orleans, Louisiana; on to Chicago, Illinois; and then to Washington, D.C.

Marie felt now was the time to settle into a new life and future. She and Kit would do a lot of talking while sorting out their new lives.

Marie N. Michell was born May 23, 1924, in Detroit, Michigan. She was 19 years old when training to become a WASP at Avenger Field.

Elizabeth Cooper "Kit" MacKethan was born December 31, 1917, in Fayetteville, North Carolina. She was 25 years old when training at Avenger Field.

CHAPTER 3

Training and Close Friendship

The Class of 44-W-2, which was Kit's and Marie's graduating class number at Avenger Field, plunged into this daily schedule:

6:00 a.m.	Reveille, wake up
6:30	Formation and roll call
7:00	Breakfast
8:00	Return to quarters
9:00	Flight/ground school/physical training
12-2:00 p.m.	Lunch
1:00	Flight/ground school/physical training
6:00	Dinner
7:00	Study, write letters
9:30	All trainees in their rooms
10:00	Lights out, taps
Saturday	Inspection in the morning, free time
	1:00 a.m. curfew
Sunday	Free time
	Lights out at 10:00 p.m.

The WASP Song

*With the wind and the sand in our eyes
And our goal placed up high in the skies
We are the WASPs who serve the Air Corps so true,
We're coming, just watch us ZOOM...down upon you!*

*On through the storm and the sun
Fly on till our mission is done
From factory to base, let the WASPs set the pace,
We're a thousand strong!*

On the left is the cover of the WASP classbook for the Class of 44-W-2. Featured on the cover is the WASP flying mascot, Fifinella (a.k.a. "Fifi"), which also appears on the WASP patch worn on the A-2 leather jackets. Fifinella refers to the female gremlins from Roald Dahl's book entitled The Gremlins, *written in 1942. The image of the Fifinella was created by Walt Disney.*

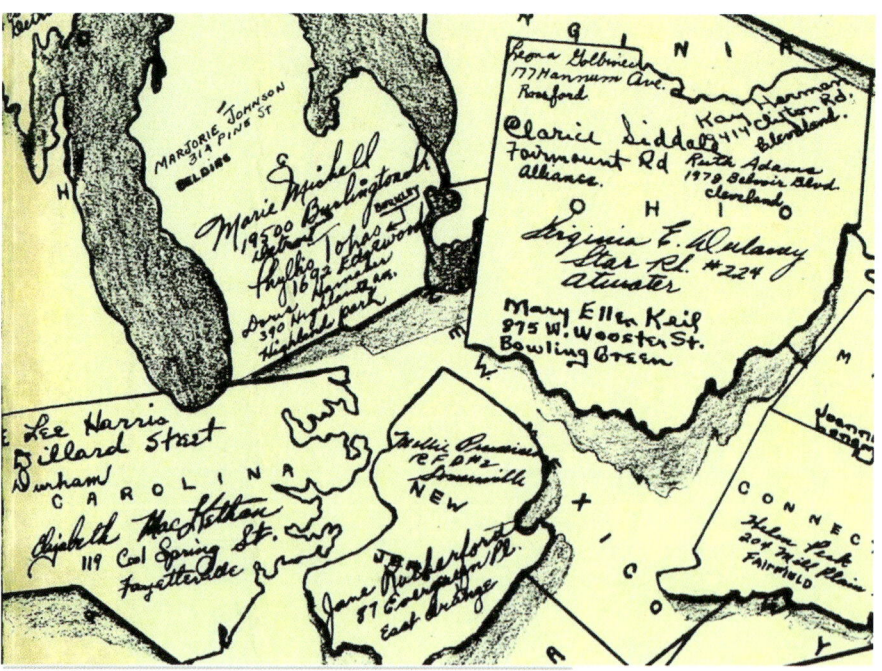

The final page in the 1944 W-2 classbook has the signatures of the trainees written in the states they were from. Marie Michell's can be seen in the middle of Michigan; Elizabeth (Kit) MacKethan's is in the middle of N. Carolina.

Originally it was just the municipal airport in Sweetwater, Texas, but then it would become the largest all-female air base in American history known as Avenger Field. The first trainees of the Women Airforce Service Pilots (WASPs) arrived on February 21, 1943. Avenger Field received its name from a local newspaper contest.

Trainees were assigned six to a room, or "bay" as it was called. They slept on army cots with thin mattresses. Each trainee had a small open closet and a footlocker to store her belongings. A latrine was between

15

two bays, providing two toilets and two showers for twelve women to share.

As fate would have it, both Marie's and Kit's surnames began with "M"; consequently, they were put together all the time in all their classes until they graduated. Wanda Langley provides many little details these women went through in her book entitled *Flying Higher*.

Marie and Kit were great buddies. They each had future aspirations that were quite similar, and they frequently shared little stories about family outings and their boyfriends. It was like they had known each other for years. Marie shared with Kit her love of Jack Hayward, explaining how she hadn't been sure about him until she went to Vanderbilt and had the opportunity to date Gray Stahlman. Now she kept thinking about Jack and didn't want to be with anyone but him. She knew other men, such as Mac her pilot instructor, but they were just nice guys who were too old for her. Only Jack had her heart. So when he proposed to her she was ecstatic and could hardly wait for the war to be over so that they could be married. They would talk to each other every chance they got, mostly at night when their studies and work was over.

1st Lt. William LaRue
Physical Director

The military officer the trainees saw most often was 1st Lt. William LaRue, the base's physical director, an energetic and humorous fellow. He conducted four hours of physical training during the week, plus one hour of close-order drill. He put the women through the same Army Air Force physical regimen that the male cadets went through. Trainees endured the grueling workouts and emerged in superb physical condition.

A private company called Aviation Enterprises, Ltd. had a government contract to provide the civilian flight and ground school instructors. It hired the many people needed to run an army base. Ground instructors taught principles of aviation and mechanics. Most were college graduates with teaching experience. They taught Morse code, navigation, simulated flight, aeronautics, math, physics, engine maintenance, and meteorology. The 400-hour curriculum was the equivalent of a graduate program. The courses were the same as those given to the male cadets, except the program was completed in less time. According to Wanda's book, in December of 1942 the Army Air Force increased the number of words per minute the male and female pilots had to send and receive in Morse code. It jumped from six words per minute to ten. After a trainee completed the Morse code requirements, she had to return every week to pass a test. If she failed, she returned to regular ground school class until she passed the exam.

BENEFIT	MEN	WOMEN
Transportation to flight school	Provided at no expense	Paid all their own expenses
If washed out of program	Assigned to other military duty	Paid their own way home
Room/board	Provided at no expense	Charged $1.65/day (Class 43-5 to end) Houston, WASP paid all expenses
Insurance	$10,000	None. Companies cancelled personal policies. WASP contributed to an emergency fund.
Uniforms	Provided	Paid over $100 for their own
Pay	$75/month	$150/month plus $26 overtime
Injury/Illness	Automatic care--no expense	Paid for their own in the beginning. Army hospitals provided for later classes
Death benefits	Automatic. Escort home. Military funeral. Family authorized to display Gold Star	$200 and a plain pine box. No military escort. Not entitled to use American flag on coffin. Survivors of WASP trainees w/ no right to display Gold Star.

Comparison of men's and women's benefits as Army Airforce pilots. More WASP statistics are available at www.wingsacrossamerica.us/wasp/stats.htm

After a week of her new routine, Marie was like a chatter-box with Kit. "I love my Grandma Kate," Marie would often say, holding a close place in her heart for her grandma. "We talked a lot after my mom and dad had divorced. She was always saying to me, 'Stop and smell the roses because life can be so hectic and frustrating.' I'd say to myself, 'Yes, Grandma, I'll slow down.'

"There was a place by Green Lake in West Bloomfield Township called the Aviation Country Club where our family would go and enjoy the golf grounds and its landing field across the street. Nothing else was around but farm houses. Then when the Great Depression hit, the Country Club lost members and eventually folded. Those were crazy times. People went from being millionaires to poverty overnight. My mother and father got a divorce one year later. That is one reason Jack and I are so perfect for each other -- we don't like divorce. We will never get a divorce. I miss him so much. I believe he's teaching at the Naval Academy at Pensacola, Florida, today. Come on, Kit, let's go to dinner."

Arm in arm the two friends went to supper, singing out loud, "*Shine on, shine on, harvest moon, for me and my guy. Snow time ain't no time to stay outdoors and spoon, so shine on, shine on, harvest moon, for me and my guy.*" Things were beginning to shape up for Marie. She'd give Jack a call this evening to find out what had transpired the day when he went to join up. They were just young girls, having fun and giggling about nothing. Silly teenagers were what her brother Roy would have called them. But she was only taking her time to smell the roses as Grandma Kate said to do.

CHAPTER 4

Tragedy Strikes

How often in life do strange things happen that cannot be explained and yet we look back and shake our heads and wonder how we got into this situation? That is precisely what happened to Marie and her fiancé.   The circumstances that had arisen between Jack and Marie were very strange. A chance happening -- perhaps one in a trillion.

Marie heard that Jack was mad at her, according to her brother Roy. Jack was stationed at Pensacola, and so was C.A. McKay. When "Mac" showed Jack his room, Jack saw Marie's high school picture signed: *To Mac with love, Marie.*

"Roy," Marie said to her brother, "I have to talk with Jack. I have to explain this to him. Mac means nothing to me. We were just good friends. He was my flight instructor, nothing more. I just wanted him to go to war with hope that there is a tomorrow, nothing more; he's too old for me anyhow. He's just a friend, nothing more."

The contention between Jack and Marie went on for several hours, and Jack's agitation would not calm down. Marie spent the rest of the night sharing her problems with Kit, but nothing seemed resolved. After a sleep-troubled night, Marie went to church with Kit the next morning. After church, Marie and Kit were talking about the strange circumstances that brought about Jack's anger.

Marie called her dad and talked to him for over an hour to see if he could give her some understanding of the situation. "You'd think that I had distributed thousands of my photographs to the entire Navy," Marie said. "Why of all places did Jack happen to be stationed as an instructor where Mac was teaching, too, in Pensacola, Florida? I don't get it! My luck has gotten really bad. According to Roy, Jack saw the same high school picture I had given to him and had signed: '*With all my Love . . . Marie.*'"

After a long conversation with her father, Marie felt no better. Then she thought her mother might have a better perspective than her dad had. It was so bewildering to Marie, who planned on marrying Jack once the war was over.

"Oh, Kit, what should I do? This is our first big quarrel. I hope this will all clear up by tomorrow. Why wouldn't it? I bet Jack must be nervous or suspicious about finding my picture in Mac's room. I simply gave Mac that picture when I graduated from high school and received my aviation license. It's just a bad misunderstanding, and by tomorrow we'll be back together again, I hope. Kit, I have to be getting my clothes laundered and my hair washed, so I'll keep myself as busy as I can. Let's just hang out for a while."

The next day someone called Marie and said, "Hey, Marie, you got a call from someone named Mac. Call him back -- he said it was important."

When she returned Mac's call, he said, "Marie, I'm sorry to have to tell you this. I have to let you know because I feel I had caused a big argument between you and Jack. He seemed to finally understand about when you gave me your picture. We talked this morning about what a good woman you are and that we were never lovers. It's not that I hadn't tried, but I had to be honest with him, and I think he understood. So I have to tell you what happened today when we went out giving lessons this morning. I can tell you now because Jack's family already knows. Jack had an accident this morning when he and his student were landing. They were both killed."

"No, NO!!" Marie screamed out. "It can't be. You have to be wrong!"

"I don't know what caused it, but when I find out I'll let you know," Mac replied. "I'm so sorry all this has happened cuz I know what a great kid you are and how miserable this news must be."

"NO, No, No, it can't be. He is the love of my life. No, No!!" she wailed.

After a day with no word, Marie received a call from Jack's father. "I'm sorry that I have to let you know this info," he said, "but Jack had an accident with the student he was teaching. They were both killed. It seems that Jack was writing down their class experience when the kid did something wrong. It happened during the easy landing they were supposed to make, and they crashed. I figured you should know, too. Tell your brother because I know that they were good friends. It takes a while for the government to process and communicate all of this, so I'll let you know when the funeral will be."

Neither Roy nor Marie was able to leave to attend Jack's funeral and grieve with his family. Marie felt that it was her fault that Jack had died because of her photograph she had given to Mac. But she had given the same one to her brother and father as well. She explained, "I always signed them, 'With all my Love, . . . Marie.'" She was convinced that Jack had died because of her carelessness. Could she ever get over this horrible event?

During this tragic time in her life, Marie would soon find herself thanking God for Kit, who had been raised in a Christian home in North Carolina and now ministered the Gospel of Jesus Christ to her. For the first time in her life, Marie understood the term being "born again," which she remembered having heard at her grandmother's church in Royal Oak, Michigan. It seemed that northern Christians were not as vociferous as the southern Christians were. Kit comforted her and told her that as a Christian she would meet her sweetheart again. "He is a Christian and will be with Jesus right now. We don't, as human beings, know much about what happens when a person dies. But you and I have to face the fact that we might experience the same sudden death that Jack encountered. I know where I will go if I die. Do you?"

Marie shook her head with tears streaming down her face, shaking her head no.

"Marie, Jesus is a gentleman and will not force himself on anybody. The devil, on the other hand, will force himself on anyone he can and give them grief. No, we have to ask Jesus into our life to be our Lord, and when he comes into our life he also forgives our sins. Some people don't think that they have sins until God comes into their life. Then they see their sins. Once Christ is in our lives, we change. It's not because we did anything on our own accord, but it's because he changed us. We didn't even realize we needed changing. Would you like to know that you will be with God when you die?"

Marie nodded her head yes. Kit had Marie ask Jesus into her life like the passage in Romans 10:8-11 tells people everywhere to do:

> *But what saith it? The Word is nigh thee, even in thy mouth, and in thy heart: that is, the Word of faith, which we preach; That if thou shalt confess with thy mouth the Lord Jesus, and shalt believe in thine heart that God hath raised him from the dead, thou shalt be saved. For with the heart man believeth unto righteousness; and with the mouth confession is made unto salvation. For the scripture saith, "Whosoever believeth on Him shall not be ashamed."*

"Kit," Marie responded, "I want you to promise me that if anything happens to me that you will go to my mother and minister to her for me. Now, Kit, I mean it. I want you to promise me if anything happens to me, you will go to be with my mother. I know how hard she will take my death. Promise me!"

"I will, Marie, but likewise you have to promise me that you'll go to my mother if anything happens to me," Kit replied.

Life was now a more serious matter to both girls. It wasn't just fun and games. A noticeable change had taken place in Marie's mind and spirit as she kept thinking of things she could have done to save Jack's life. The thought of her own future life was uncertain. If life had been so short for Jack, what guarantee does anyone really have? Death and its heavy consequences were something new to her.

After a week of profound mourning, Marie still found tears welling up in her eyes and was finding it difficult to change her thoughts and mood. There was such an empty spot inside of her. It was not as if she had lost her mother or father. But she still felt numbness in her life that she had never experienced before. Sometimes situations arose when she found herself saying she needed to let Jack know about it, or she figured that he would get a kick out of whatever just happened. But then came the stark realization that Jack was no more.

CHAPTER 5

Rugged But Right

Things were going so fast nowadays that it was hard keeping up with her old life. She was so busy that she had not kept in touch with her mother or dad. She would see her brother periodically, or at least talk with him on the phone when she felt lonely.

Marie still wept many tears at times, having wanted Jack to be proud of her. She was sure he lost his focus when the accident occurred because of her stupid signed photograph. Whenever she thought about the crash, the tears flowed again from her light green eyes.

Marie, Kit and all the trainees at Avenger Field were busy beyond belief, learning physics and higher mathematics and lots of other things. Marie and Kit had an advantage over the other students since they had been Link Trainer instructors before coming to Avenger Field. The Link Trainer gave the students the ability to fly at night or in a storm by using the planes instrument panel. Wanda Langley explains the flight simulation, this way: The trainee was shut into the Link for an hour or so for instruction. Inside the student sat before an airplane instrument panel. She had controls to operate and a chart to consult. The instructor sat outside and had a similar but larger chart spread on a big table. The instructor gave directions by radio. As the trainee "flew," her reactions were recorded on the outside chart by a large stylus. At the end of the lesson, the operator showed the student what mistakes she had made and whether she had arrived at the correct destination.

In the Link Trainer, the student had to learn to fly by radio beam to land in the right place. In the 1940s, the United States was crisscrossed with radio stations, each having its own frequency and beams. Some of the sending stations were located at or near local airports. Every station had a different Morse code to identify its location. For example, to locate

Cleveland, Ohio, by instruments, the student found the Morse code for the Cleveland beacon on her map and tuned into the radio frequency as she approached the city. If she correctly tuned her receiver, she heard the sounds of dot-dash (Morse code for the letter "A") and dash-dot (letter "N") which overlapped to produce a steady hum. She was now flying "on the beam." If she were to fly toward the airport, the hum grew louder as she approached. When she heard no sound, it meant she was right over the Cleveland airport. She had entered the "cone of silence." Had this cone-shaped area been visible, it would have become larger as it rose; thus, no matter how high the plane was, the pilot hit silence if she were over the correct destination.

At this point, the trainee could begin her descent. If she had calculated her altitude correctly with her airspeed, she saw the Cleveland runway below her plane when she broke through to clear sky. If she could not find the runway and attempted to land, she "crashed." Wreaths were hung on the Link Trainer room walls for those who had symbolically died during their Link Trainer lessons. The instruction was intense, frustrating claustrophobic work.

But it was absolutely necessary for trainees to master Morse code and instrument training before going on to the real thing. Needless to say, all the other classes that they had to master in six months were grueling as well.

For work uniforms the ladies were assigned *men's* coveralls, called "zoot suits," sizes 44 and up. Their seats swished as they walked. For dress uniform they had to buy khaki slacks, matching caps and white blouses. Because of the girls' long hair, Director Jacqueline Cochran required them to wear white turbans. Two rules were strictly enforced: No alcohol on the base and no dating the instructors.

They had no social life whatsoever between lessons and flying. Their time really was not their own. Many of the girls who were good pilots would wash out for any misdemeanor. The officers were tough on the cadets, but the cadets respected them for it. The majority were morally good girls that believed in saving themselves from promiscuous activity until they were married. Most came from some sort of religious background, had hardworking parents and were proud Americans. They believed in God and doing things the right way. People's beliefs were not any more complicated than that.

Although people usually never mentioned God much or discussed theology, it was very common to say and hear things like "My God," "Oh, God," and "God, why didn't we think of that?" The word "God" was used a lot that way despite parents instructing their kids not to use the name of the Lord in vain. It was really just a popular expression, like some of the songs being sung with risqué lyrics that meant nothing to the people singing them.

Jackie Cochran would not tolerate such risqué songs on the base. As innocent as the ladies were, however, they felt a bit entitled to be able to sing them. One of the popular ones was called "Rugged But Right."

Rugged But Right

I just called up to tell you that I'm rugged but right!
A rambling woman, a gambling woman, drunk every night.
A porterhouse steak three times a day for my board,
That's more than any decent gal in town can afford!
I've got a big electric fan to keep me cool while I eat,
A tall and handsome man to keep me warm while I sleep!
I'm a rambling woman, a gambling woman and BOY am I tight!
I just called up to tell you that I'm rugged but right!
HO-HO-HO—Rugged but right!

CHAPTER 6

Christmas 1943

Work was hard, and the weather started getting worse. Before they would know it, Christmas would be there. It was getting a little chilly outside for sunbathing, which they all loved to do. The intense heat was long gone and their zoot suits felt good in the chilly weather. They planned to enjoy the Christmas holiday. Little trees were put up with some girls looping little colored buttons together to string on their small trees. Some strung popcorn. Marie found a miserable looking old tree at the picked-over Christmas tree lot. When she asked if they would sell it to her, they told her she could have it. She quickly grabbed it. The attendant had cut the top of the tree off, and that was what she had set up in their bay. It made a beautiful tree, just the right size for them. Then she went off to the local "dime" store, either Kresge or Woolworths, both popular for all the little things one needed. The store had some earrings for a dime, so she bought several.

The officers said for each of the girls to arrange a skit of some sort for a Christmas program. Marie remembered a little dance number she performed as a kid with the Dorothy Dorben Dancers during the Christmas season; it included some Nutcracker and Swan Lake dances. Kit and Marie had fun with that. But the festivities made her feel a bit lonely, too. She naturally still missed Jack, so she prayed that Jack would enjoy their Christmas fun even though she knew he was in heaven with the angels. Kit told her she would meet him when she died and went to heaven, and she knew a lot more about the Bible than Marie did, so she believed her.

Marie made sure to call her family and tell them all the things she and the girls were able to do now and how well things were going. She told them they were all praying for snow for Christmas because it was getting so bleak outside. Most people laughed when she told them they were praying for a White Christmas. She realized that the base was in Sweetwater, Texas, and they seldom if ever got more than snow flurries there. But back home in Royal Oak, Michigan, at Grandma Kate Jackson's, she always prayed for snow at Christmas time, and they usually got it.

The sun had not been shining much lately, and most of the girls were a little homesick. No matter what, though, they would carry on because they were so determined to make the WASPs a success. Marie loved every time she was able to go up in her plane. She would feel close to God the moment she was up in the sky. That was hard for her to explain to her brother when they talked about it. She felt so free, so limitless. Oh, it was such a wonderful experience.

The most amazing thing occurred the next morning. Everyone was awestruck when they woke up Christmas Day to mounds and mounds of snow. It wasn't just flurries, but piles of windblown snow all around instead. Everyone kept shaking their heads in disbelief. Without hesitation they did what red-blooded American girls do: they went outside and threw snowballs at each other, Christmas Day 1943. Due to the weather, all flying stopped until conditions improved.

One week later, on January 1, 1944, another new snowfall arrived. This meant the pilots had to use their Link Trainer experience right away. The last two weeks in January of 1944 gave them the opportunity for their last training phase: cross-country navigation, and short, medium and long distance flight. Their newly-learned skills were being put to the test, and this was a golden opportunity to fly the aircraft under a variety of conditions.

The temperatures were so cold during this freeze that Kit and Marie went to bed with their zoot suits on. Any excuse to go into town to warmer facilities was pounced on. The month of January was miserable, but the cadets hung in there. They would not complain for fear that they might wash out. They were determined to be good sports about everything. Marie had a chance to talk to her brother on January 12, his birthday, and he cheered her up with a few jokes.

CHAPTER 7

Graduation

The girls were very fortunate to have such a brilliant leader as Jackie Cochran organizing the WASPs. She had a gifted sense of style. She paid to have her girls in designer uniforms. She chose a dark blue wool that she called Santiago blue. General George Marshall, Army Chief of Staff, selected the Santiago blue fine wool and guaranteed payment for the uniforms, about $175. That included the beret, jacket and skirt. The girls had to spend about $100 for their shirt, shoes, ties and undergarments. This was a hardship for some of the women because their pay of $150/month with $26 overtime had to cover their room and board and all their other expenditures. Some helped those who needed it. They were all sisters working for America. A sisterhood of WASPs.

March 11, 1944, was graduation day for Marie and Kit. Seven Army generals landed at Avenger Field. General Henry H. ("Hap") Arnold, who was the commanding general of the United States Army Air Forces, was their commencement speaker. He said:

> *I am looking forward to the day when Women Airforce Service Pilots take the place of practically all AAF pilots in the U.S. for the duration of the war. The WASPs are doing an effective job of delivering aircraft in the U.S. from the smallest planes to big fighters, bombers, and transports. They fill the need for professional non-combat service in the country and Canada. For example, the Training 5 Command uses many women pilots to ferry airplanes to and from certain bases for major repair or overhaul.*

> *However, in recent months the WASPs have assumed additional duties—towing targets in gunnery schools, acting as copilots on night searchlight missions and the like.*

Women pilots also are flying some of the weather planes which take meteorologists aloft. Indeed, this organization has come to serve a variety of useful purposes in the Army Air Forces organization. We can use and probably will continue to use as many WASPs as we can turn out for these non-combat duties.

We are proud of you and welcome you as part of the Army Air Forces.

After giving his speech, General Hap Arnold handed out special awards to some members of 44-W-2 for their leadership abilities. As Mrs. Deaton rose to call each graduate, she dropped the list of names. When she picked them up they no longer were in order, and General Hap Arnold went on to pin all the remaining girls. Jackie Cochran said, "Never mind, General, you don't have to do that." But General Hap Arnold replied, "Never mind, Jackie, I enjoy doing this." Thus he pinned all forty-nine graduates. This thrilled Marie and Kit. It was such an unexpected blessing for the whole group.

The graduation ceremony ended with the singing of "The Star-Spangled Banner." Everyone then moved outside to the flight line for final review. Wanda Langley provides further details of all the activities in her book entitled *Flying Higher*. She has done an excellent job in relating all the things these women went through.

After the graduates went outside, they continued singing. Soon the Class of 44-W-2 broke into a spirited rendition of the infamous and forbidden "Rugged But Right." They were all so excited now that all the hard work was over with for a while.

"Mom came to our graduation ceremony, and I hadn't seen her for six months," Marie told her brother. "That made me so happy. But I didn't want to go back home with her. Even though we had a ten-day leave, because of losing Jack, my emotions were still too raw. Mother understood; she's that kind of mom. I love her so much -- I'll make it up to her somehow."

Marie decided to go to her dad's summer home on Walloon Lake in Michigan. He opened it ahead of time just for her. She could fish for walleyes and relax. That time of the spring was still rather cold. One month later, though, it would be perfect.

When Marie returned to Avenger Field, she was notified that she had been assigned to the Fifth Ferry Group at Love Field, Dallas, Texas, and could be transferred to other bases as needed. At this point the women were in the military system and subject to transfer, just as the male pilots were. The first thing she wanted to do was call her brother, who could help her feel better and not alone. She didn't know exactly where Roy was, but when she discovered he was at Hensley Field in Dallas, she was delighted. How nice God was to Marie, to place Roy so close to her at such a lonely time in her life. At Christmas time Roy had been in Athens, Georgia, but now he was here with her, which made it really nice.

Marie was thrilled that Roy could come over once in a while, have a Coke together, and talk about Mom, Grandma and old times. Roy was now in a Naval training program as a midshipman, learning meteorology and weather conditions. The third time Roy came to visit, Marie introduced him to Captain Hampton C. Robinson III, a new friend of hers. He was a flight surgeon, living in Texas. "Hamp," as he was called, was a different type of personality than Jack had been. Jack had been the athletic type who loved sports and was a big man, whereas Hamp was a smaller man and, as a doctor, rather more sensitive in nature.

CHAPTER 8

Surprising News

Marie was assigned to the Fifth Ferry Group at Love Field near Dallas on March 22, 1944. After having had time to spend with her father, she managed to spend some time with her mother as she had promised her. But the real excitement came when she found out that her almost-twin brother was stationed at Hensley Field in Dallas, and Kit, her best friend, was there, too.

Wanda Langley's book *Flying Higher* gives great detail on what and how the girls were paid and where they would eat if they got back before the restaurant closed. Every flyer had a Pilot's Information File of regulations, procedures, flying safety, and up-to-date memoranda. When they checked in they took an oath of office, filled out forms and were assigned to Delphine Bohn, their squadron commander. They were to report at 8:00 a.m. to Delphine Bohn's office and receive their flight instructions.

After graduating as WASPs, both Kit and Marie went to Army Air Forces Strategic Command School in Orlando, Florida, for the month of April 1944. Jackie Cochran had hoped this advanced training to American and Allied military officers would eventually lead the WASPs to be commissioned as military officers. Unfortunately, the Costello Bill, HR4219, which would have officially made the WASP a woman's service in the USAAF, was defeated in Congress by nineteen votes on June 21, 1944, despite General Arnold's backing.

For the next month of training, which lasted eight hours a day, six days a week, they attended classes in Military Law: Principles of Leadership, Military Customs, Intelligence Operations, Survival Skills, Advanced Meteorology, and Advanced Navigation. They endured physical training and drills. They also viewed air battle films, learned how radar systems worked, and increased their use of weapons skills.

The Orlando school included international students. They met officers from Great Britain, France, Turkey, and the Soviet Union. The most interesting were the Soviet women pilots, who had demonstrated tremendous bravery and valor. One of them had shot down seventeen German aircraft.

After Marie's training in Orlando was complete, she returned to Dallas. A number of things were on her mind, including her future in the military and her relationship with Hampton Robinson. She wrote her dad on August 6, 1944, on Officers Club stationary from Love Field, Texas, with a photograph of three women walking under a banner imprinted with the words "Ferrying Group".

August 6, 1944

Dear Dad,

    I received your letter this morning and since I have a few moments now thought I'd answer, 'cause I don't know when I'll be able to find time again. I returned to Dallas last week to find things in a very sad state of affairs. It appears that Washington is all upset because a few civilian pilots, who wouldn't join up when they were called, are very eager to join the Ferry Command now instead of going into the walking Army and are demanding that the WASPs be kicked out. They not only didn't want us in the Army, but they began articles in all the papers stating what a poor investment we turned out to be, etc.

    So, slowly but surely they're getting us transferred and kicked out of the Ferry Command. It's gotten to the point where none of the girls feel badly about resigning anymore. If they don't want us, OK. Anyway, about 50 gals from Dallas are being transferred sometime this week, and none of us knows where we're going. We do know, however, that we will be working for the training command, and that they have too many pilots as it is. I just hope our new jobs aren't a waste of time.

    Guess what I'm wearing on my left hand?? My flight surgeon flew down to see me last week -- I was out on a trip as usual -- but managed to get back a day before he had to leave so we became engaged. By the way, his name's Capt. Hampton C. Robinson. I don't know when we'll get married; a lot depends upon my new base and whether he has to go to the Southwest Pacific again. But don't worry, I'll keep you posted, you're on my priority 1 list!

Dallas is terribly hot now; perspiration is running all over the place, it's almost impossible to sleep at night. How I wish I could spend a few weeks up at Walloon with you. Mmmmmmmmmmmmmmmmmmmm that would be wonderful ...."

I'll send you my new address as soon as I know it. In the meantime you can write me here.

Lotsa love,
Marie

Oil painting on canvas of Marie Michell Robinson by T.C. Christman, based on photograph Marie sent to her father, Roy Michell

Oil painting on canvas of Marie Michell Robinson by T.C. Christman, based on photograph Marie sent to her father, Roy Michell

CHAPTER 9

Special Correspondence

Major Robinson wrote to Marie's father on August 10, 1944:

Dear Mr. Michell --

 For some time I have intended writing you a letter, but words simply set down on paper form a poor substitute for a cordial handshake as a preface to becoming acquainted. Since I have been unable to avail myself of an opportunity to come to Detroit, however, perhaps a letter will serve the purpose until we can meet personally.

 If Marie has spoken of me in her letters to you then it will come as no surprise that this note owes its existence to my feelings toward your daughter, whom I met in Dallas shortly after returning from a two-year tour of duty in the South and Central Pacific areas.

 It is probably superfluous for me so say that I'm very much in love with Marie. Last week I flew to Dallas and on August the 4th asked her to marry me. She is at present wearing my ring. I would like, sir, to have your consent to our marriage and your blessing.

 Since you do not know me I can appreciate fully your feelings in this matter and hope that in the near future I can fly to Detroit in order that we may meet and become better acquainted.

 If Marie has not told you perhaps you would be interested in knowing that my home is in Texas, that after finishing the University of Texas, I attended Baylor University, College of Medicine, in Dallas, and after graduating took some postgraduate work in surgery. In the summer of 1941, I volunteered for active duty and have been in the Army since that time. To that I might add that my racial extraction is English and French and you would have a very brief sketch of the man who is asking for your daughter's hand in marriage.

 We have not decided upon a date; that I shall leave for Marie to decide. We have considered all the possibilities and problems presented by the war and its attending circumstances. To exactly predict the future is of course impossible, but to accurately evaluate present conditions can be done quite satisfactorily considering that all things are a bit uncertain. Marriage at this time may appear inopportune, but certainly should not appear injudicious.

Marie has met both my mother and my father and it goes without saying that both feel as keenly about her as they do about their older son and would welcome her to our family.

In the hope that I may have your consent and approval, I am

Yours most sincerely,
Hampton Robinson, Jr.

Marie's dad was so eager to reply to Hampton's proper letter to him.

August 16, 1944

Dear Hampton --

Marie has inked to me that she was extremely interested in a certain flight surgeon, so your good letter was not too much of a surprise.

As you undoubtedly surmise, I am deeply fond of and proud of my daughter and of the progress she has made in the last couple of years, and naturally am most anxious for her happiness. I believe Marie, tho' still quite young, is fully capable of judging for herself as to the man she chooses to marry, and so while I was immensely pleased to hear from you personally, her own acceptance of you, plus a recent remark from Roy Jr. that you were 'tops" gives me confidence that this should prove a happy marriage for both of you.

I presume that after the war you will be practicing in Texas? Or is it too much to hope that you might be locating somewhere in the North? Perhaps that might be a bit selfish, but you see, Marie has been so far away for the past two or three years that I have only had a few quick glimpses of her.

Your activities in the South Pacific should prove invaluable to you later on when you re-establish yourself in your profession, and tho' there is still a very major job to be done before our country is in position to resume some semblance of normal living, I do sincerely hope that you will not be called back to active service at the front again. It would seem that two years is a pretty good stretch, especially when there are probably so many others available. I had greatly hoped that Marie could have spent a little time with us this summer here at Walloon Lake where it is so restful, but that has not materialized. Maybe next summer both of you can be here -- it does not seem possible that our country will still be at war a year from now. There is very little social life here, but we have grand air, sunlight, bathing and other relaxing opportunities.

Your frank letter impressed me very much indeed. As you say, it is difficult to aptly put into a letter the things we can say during personal contact and frankly I do so hope you can make a flight to Detroit very soon for I am anxious to know well the man who will be Marie's husband, and I think too, you ought to know her father!

Marie has doubtless told you that I look at most all human relations from the practical viewpoint. While she may not have had a luxurious childhood, she really has had practically everything she has ever wanted, except possibly her own horses, car and plane. However, I do think Marie is a most sensible girl with a good sense of humor and well balanced, and that especially after the rugged training of the past year she should be able to adapt herself to almost any condition, financial or otherwise which might arise in the course of your married life.

Marie is one grand girl and I want her marriage throughout to be filled with the same kind of enthusiasm and success that she has experienced in her aviation activities. I am sure that you are the one that can kindle and nourish those attributes.

I am writing Marie that you have my approval even tho' I have not met you face to face. Personally, I do hope you Hampton and Marie will delay until you know for sure that you Hampton will not be called back into combat service, but I also hope that you will be able to "ground" her soon, or at least discontinue her hazardous flying, but whatever Marie decides, as to your wedding date, you shall both have my blessing!

Marie's Grandmother and Mrs. Michell join me in wishing you the best of luck and happiness!

Very Sincerely,
Roy Michell

P.S. I may remain here at Walloon until August 25th, or a few days later if the good weather holds out. However, should you be flying to Detroit, and I hope you can before that date, wire me here and I will meet you in Detroit whenever you can come.

As mentioned in the above letter to Hampton, Marie's dad then wrote to Marie about the engagement.

Marie dear --

So you're going to take the great leap! Well, I didn't suppose that a gal as sweet and attractive as you are could be expected to continue running around unattached for long! Congratulations and happy landings to you, sweetheart!

I have received a very nice letter from your fiancé, Hampton. (By the way, what should I call him for short? "Hamp" or "Doc"?) His letter, plus Roy's, okay, plus the fact that you ought to know your men by now, gives me confidence that he must be a "right guy," but gosh I wish he would fly to Detroit so we could sit down for a good old talk.

He said he was leaving the wedding date "for Marie to decide." I know that when two folks "get to thinking about marryin'" the date is usually set "sooner" rather than "later". In your letter too, you said, "a lot depends upon my new base, and whether he has to go back to the Southwest Pacific." My dear, let your ole' man urge you, if there is ever any chance that he may go back to the combat area, to wait until he returns. I urge this strictly from a practical standpoint for your own future's sake. If you wait, you will have all the rest of your lives to be married together, anyway. But if you jump into it before he returns to the front, and anything should happen to him, you'd be a widow the rest of your life, and my dear that isn't the grandest of outlooks, especially for one of your tender years. Think it over.

I have urged him to fly to Detroit for I sure would like to meet my prospective new son! Also, I think he should know your dad too. Suggest you likewise urge it. He could stay at the house with us, of course.

I was much impressed with his frankness and his respectful attitude. It certainly indicates a gentlemanly background, which should contribute much toward a happy life with him, from that angle.

By the way, what is his religion (if any)? Not that it would make any difference, when you are in love, but I am curious, since he touched upon everything but that, and finances.

Incidentally, can he support you in the manner to which you have been accustomed? I assume he will be returning to Dallas to practice, but most young doctors I have known are seldom in the dough, for their first few years at least. I presume you have talked that over and that you are satisfied to go along on whatever basis he can support you. Just in case you aren't familiar with that set up – it's awfully important, dear.

Anyway, I have answered his letter as best I could, affixing my favorite Okay, and sprinkled our paternal blessing on you both.

Regarding your future work – if it doesn't suit you why don't you skip it? You've sure had a strenuous year training and flying all over these here United States and I feel you have contributed your share in the country's war effort!

I expect to be here until about Aug. 25 – if the weather holds out. (Maybe Sept 1ˢᵗ) then back in Detroit. (If Hampton were to fly to Det. before then, I would go down especially to meet him.)

Let me know your new address pronto, dear. Betty joins me in wishing you utmost happiness in your great adventure!

Loads of Love,
Dad

CHAPTER 10

Celestial Flight

Whereas Kit was sent to Cochran Field (not named after Jackie) in Mason, Georgia, to test trainer planes, Marie was sent to Victorville Army Airfield in California to fly training missions for bombardier students. When Marie arrived there on September 18, 1944, she was one of eight WASPs at the base, which was under the command of Col. Earl Robbins. At first the base officials were reluctant about WASP transfers until they found out the eight women had over 500 flying hours each. The Victorville Army Airfield was located on the edge of the Mojave Desert, an ideal location for bomb training.

After Marie was transferred to Victorville, she continued to see newly-promoted Major Hampton Robinson, who was stationed in Reno, Nevada. She rode transport planes to meet him at Lake Tahoe on the weekends. "Hamp" also came to visit her at Victorville, California. They were an attractive couple who kept to themselves. They would eat dinner together at the mess hall, take walks, and sit outside on the barracks steps and talk.

In late September, Marie wrote the following letter to her father:

September 30th
Happy Birthday Dad!
 Wish I were there to plant a big birthday "burner"! I made a trip into San Bernardino the other day and found a little present for you, hope that it gets there on time and that you like it.
 Golly, this base is very nice, even tho it's out in the middle of nowhere. I'm in school learning how to fly ships on bombing missions and very shortly will fly bombardiers on practice spins, dropping 100 lb. bombs. It's lots of fun, but we work from 0530 (5:30 a.m.) till 10 at night and really drop into bed at night.

> *I expect another temporary transfer next month, and if it actually comes about will resign at that time -- getting tired of being kicked from one base to another. Getting kinda lonesome for my man, too; think I'll get married one of these days! By the way, Hamp's a Major now.*
> *Please tell Grandma that I'm thinking of her and will write soon.*
> *Lots of love*
> *Marie*

On Monday, October 2, 1944, Marie's new roommate had been invited to go up with a friend on the B-25, a twin-engine medium bomber. The B-25 had gained fame as the bomber used in the Doolittle Raid on April 18, 1942. Lieutenant Colonel Jimmy Doolittle had led sixteen B-25s in an attack on mainland Japan, four months after the bombing of Pearl Harbor.

Marie's new roommate suffered from a terrible toothache that day, so Marie asked if she could go in her place. The pilot for the flight was 1st Lt. George Rosado from San Diego, California. Marie flew in the copilot's seat, and the crew chief, S/Sgt. Gordon Walker from Fossil, Oregon, sat behind them. They took off at 3:00 p.m. Twenty minutes later the plane crashed and burned approximately 25 miles west of Victorville AAB.

A B-25 twin-engine medium bomber

Records indicate that two eyewitnesses flying nearby in Bell P-39's stated that they saw the B-25D stall and then enter a spin from which there was no recovery. Crash trucks were able to drive to the accident site. When they arrived, they discovered there were no survivors. After the completion of the coroner's report, the wreckage was removed from the site.

Major Robinson accompanied Marie's ashes back home to Michigan for burial. Her family was scattered across the country: Marie's father was in Michigan; her mother lived in Washington, D.C.; her stepfather served in the military overseas; and her brother Roy was stationed at Wildwood Naval Air Station, a base in New Jersey, as an aerographer.

Kit was at Cochran Field in Georgia. When she heard of Marie's death and tried to get details on the funeral arrangements, all she learned was that the memorial service would be at White Chapel Cemetery in Troy, Michigan.

According to the www.arlingtoncemetery.net website, Kit completed her test flying duties for the day while waiting for military transportation to Michigan for Marie's memorial service. "As she soared upward amidst the soft fair weather cumulus clouds, she fantasized that her friend was there. She recalled the happy days training when she, Marie and sky were one -- on playful silver wings. But Marie was not there." Kit "landed and in a secluded spot in the Operations Room she penned "Celestial Flight" in words that seemed to come from a Source other than herself."

Kit travelled to Washington, D.C., to be with Marie's mother Ruth to fulfill the promise she and Marie had made to each other if some tragedy like this ever occurred. She typed out and shared with Ruth the words she knew God had inspired her to say, words that reflected the drive and hopes within these brave young women. This touching poem, so poignant and heartfelt, would subsequently be adopted by the WASP organization and read at the passing of each pilot.

Kit and Marie enjoying the thrill of flying

CELESTIAL FLIGHT

She is not dead –
But only flying higher,
Higher than she's flown before,
And earthly limitations
Will hinder her no more.
There is no service ceiling,
Or any fuel range,
And there is no anoxia,
Or need for engine change.

Thank God that now her flight can be
To heights her eyes had scanned,
Where she can race with comets,
And buzz the rainbow's span.
For she is universal
Like courage, love, and hope,
And all free, sweet emotions
Of vast and godly scope.

And understand a pilot's fate
Is not the thing she fears,
But rather sadness left behind,
Your heartbreak and your tears.

So all you loved ones, dry your eyes,
Yes, it is wrong that you should grieve,
For she would love your courage more,
And she would want you to believe
She is not dead.
You should have known
That she is only flying higher,
Higher than she's ever flown.

Marie's brother Roy travelled from New Jersey to Washington, D.C., and then accompanied his bereaved mother and Kit to Royal Oak, Michigan, where Marie's Grandma Kate Jackson lived. White Chapel Cemetery was located only a few miles from there.

The funeral was small with less than a dozen people in attendance. It was then that the family first heard of Marie's secret marriage to Major Hamp Robinson III. The couple had planned a large wedding after the war. Marie knew it was what her mother Ruth would have wanted.

A few days after the memorial service, Marie's father received the birthday letter his 20-year-old daughter had mailed to him prior to her crash. How difficult that was -- Marie had been the joy of his life. Perhaps time does heal wounds to some extent, however. He would later be blessed with a granddaughter from Marie's brother. The child was named Cheryl Marie Michell. Roy Michell Sr. established a scholarship fund at the University of Michigan in memory of his daughter. The daughter of one 44-W-2 WASP attended college with the benefit of this scholarship.

CHAPTER 11

Discovery in the Mojave Desert

The story doesn't end there. Over sixty years later – in February 2005 – some amateur aviation archaeologists revisited the crash site. A year earlier they had learned of the 1944 B-25 plane crash involving Marie, and with growing determination they began the difficult search for the wreckage area. The Air Force provided a copy of the crash report, which furnished some clues on where to look, but there was nothing that gave a specific location.

Crash site of B-25D #41-30114 in Mojave Desert. The picture was taken by the Project Remembrance Team in 2005, over 60 years after the plane crashed and killed all three on board.

When the "wreck finders," as they called themselves, searched the Internet and discovered Kit's poem written for Marie along with several photos of Marie, they became engrossed with the endeavor.

Through persistence, David Schurhammer, a construction worker from Fullerton, California, who read military airplane crash reports in his free time, and G. Pat Macha, a retired high school geography and history teacher from Huntington Beach, California, who shared the same passion for aircraft wrecks, succeeded in their efforts. With help from Mike Lyons, Macha was finally able to find what remained of #41-30114. His son, Pat J. Macha, joined the search team as well. They found the spot where Marie Michell, Lt. Rosado and S/Sgt. Walker lost their lives.

As the amateur archeologists scouted the terrain, they recovered Marie's bracelet, her Bulova watch, her wedding band and her uniform collar insignia. A number of items are often left behind by the original response team because it has little time to find everything, pressed foremost to recover the bodies and as much of the plane as possible. Extended time for a thorough search for smaller artifacts was especially lacking during WWII when the number of crashes was high due to all the training being conducted.

A few of Marie's artifacts were found on the desert floor by the Project Remembrance Team. A crash site is left mostly undisturbed, except for personal items that are returned to the family. The location is not disclosed to the public to prevent souvenir hunters from ransacking it.

In May 2005, Schurhammer contacted Marie's brother Roy, telling him of what they found. Roy was stunned about the news. He was aware of such a bracelet, however, because his mother Ruth had given both Marie and him a bracelet with their own name engraved on it when they each went off to war.

Roy later responded, "All of this seems like a movie, but the ending wasn't really the end. To know that she was wearing [the recovered items] that day. Well, I don't know what to think."

Gary Pat Macha is founder of Project Remembrance, a volunteer organization "dedicated to facilitate requests of next of kin who wish to learn more about the loss of loved ones in aircraft accidents, including crash site visitations." Next of kin are not charged for services rendered by team members. Their website, which has information on many crash sites, is www.aircraftwrecks.com. You can see more pictures, get more details, and watch a brief video of them at this particular location, too.

When the Project Remembrance Team revisited the crash site with members of Lt. George Rosado's family on November 12, 2005, the family placed a memorial plaque there in tribute of all three people who died in service for their country. Along with the names of the deceased were two stanzas from "Crossing the Bar" by English poet Alfred, Lord Tennyson. It reads:

> *Sunset and evening star,*
> *And one clear call for me*
> *I hope to see my Pilot face to face*
> *When I have crossed the bar*

This memorial plaque was installed and secured in cement on the desert floor in 2005. Some of S/Sgt. Walker's family came and paid their respects at the site on January 12, 2013.

CHAPTER 12

A Niece's Mission

After reading Wanda Langley's book *Flying Higher* in 2003, Marie's niece, Cheryl Marie Michell, came alive with her aunt's story. She was determined to do her part in making certain her aunt received the proper honors she deserved. Even if it were decades after the crash.

Cheryl Marie Michell holds the photo of her aunt, Marie Michell Robinson, who inspired her with such pioneering spirit and amazing accomplishments

When Cheryl learned from her father a few years later about Marie's personal effects found in the Mojave Desert, she got in touch with officials regarding the Women in Military Service for America Memorial (WIMSA), a memorial established by the U.S. federal government which honors women who have served in the United States Armed Forces. The memorial, dedicated on October 18, 1997, is located outside the gates of Arlington National Cemetery. The Michell family donated Marie's recovered items to the memorial.

Cheryl was now on her way to doing something she had always felt she needed to do. If in a lifetime there is ever a need to be heard or to be of help, she had now found her mission. These ladies needed her to further their cause – and she was able and willing. She forged ahead, making many new friends and even locating some WASPs that had been lost in time. She would even visit them and their families, if at all possible.

One of the WASPs that Cheryl met had even made her a bracelet like Marie's. She became very involved with the few pioneering women from WWII that were left. She loved these women and felt such a kinship to them. She marveled at their abilities.

Time passed, but Cheryl persisted in her mission. Since Marie never received a formal burial back in 1944, for Memorial Day in 2013 Cheryl made all the necessary arrangements for getting her aunt a well-deserved tribute with full military honors. She arranged for an honor guard salute, with trumpet, guns and lots of flags at the ceremony. She even had roses for the children to place on their great-aunt's grave.

The *Detroit Free Press* gave a wonderful, front-page story honoring the 20-year-old WASP who died while serving her country. In the article, Marie's brother Roy – Cheryl's father – noted, "To Marie, flying was just a natural thing. She loved it. I figured, right from the start, she was a better pilot than I was."

The caption under Cheryl's picture on the front page quoted Cheryl: "I've got her blood running in my veins, and it makes me feel more empowered."

The article also featured a photograph of a replica of the Congressional Gold Medal that was awarded to Marie and her fellow WASPs three years earlier on March 10, 2010.

This Congressional Gold Medal was signed into law by President Obama on July 1, 2009; the newly-designed medal was publically presented to the WASPs at the Capitol by Congress on March 10, 2010.

For Memorial Day 2013, Cheryl Michell arranged a ceremony with full military honors for her aunt, Marie Michell Robinson, who was buried in Block "I", Section 14064, Space 5, in White Chapel Cemetery in Troy, Michigan, nearly 70 years earlier without honors bestowed. Flags and roses surrounded the grave.

Cheryl's plans for the event were meticulous. In addition to the 400 large American flags that lined the cemetery's roadway, another 37 smaller American flags surrounded her aunt's grave to represent the 37 other WASPs who had died in service. A large poster of Marie in uniform rested on a nearby display stand, and a bronze wreath medal with Marie's name above a star in the center was on display by the grave as well. A podium was placed in front for the speakers, and rows of seats were arranged under a canopy to provide shelter for those who would hear Marie's incredible story and who had come to honor the brave young pioneer. Cheryl provided a rose for each of the Michell grandchildren, great-nieces and -nephews of Marie to place upon her marker.

Perhaps the most special part of the occasion was when Cheryl recited Kit's poem. Loving words written nearly seven decades earlier were so fitting and moving once again.

EPILOGUE

The Author's Perspective

Life does not happen the way we want it, but the way God has planned it to be, for HIS reasons. As time goes on we then can see what wonderful results he brings about because HE did it HIS WAY.

This is a story about two particular women in the history of the United States. One was a young girl who wanted to help her country as a pilot during WWII, and the other was a niece of hers -- my daughter -- who established a special after-death bond with her pioneering aunt. Neither of them planned on being in history books. But because I am a longtime member of D.A.R. (Daughters of the American Revolution) who believes so strongly in history, I had to finish this true tale of an aunt and her niece.

I feel a deep desire to write the books I have written for various reasons, one of them being for our descendants. We women have stories to tell that our mothers and grandmothers have told us, but when we go to be with Jesus, who will tell our grandmothers' stories if we have not written them down for posterity? Thus I felt compelled to finish this story that my daughter Cheri asked me to finish as she was dying.

Cheri first became interested in her aunt in 2003 at Christmastime when I sent her the book *Flying Higher* by Wanda Langley with a note:

Dear Cheri,
This is a story about your Aunt Marie. She died during World War II, before you were born.
Love, Mom

P.S. WOW! That was over 60 years ago.

When Cheri was growing up, I did not talk to her about her Aunt Marie or my brother, her Uncle Lloyd Firman "Buddy" Clawson, who also was a pilot killed during WWII. The tragedies that took place in 1944 were difficult to deal with then, and our family was busy afterward with a number of other important matters, as well as simply growing up and handling day-to-day life issues.

But when the time finally came to talk about Marie and celebrate her achievements, Cheri was excited about it all and dove in wholeheartedly. It was an adventure for her, learning what young women endured in society not so long ago and doing what she could for them in appreciation. It was truly a labor of love working with the WASPs. The Memorial Day tribute to Marie in 2013 was a highlight for Cheri.

Cheri already had been dealing with some personal struggles at this point in her life, but soon she was confronting other serious problems. She had been diagnosed with MS while she lived in Florida. She then discovered she had liver cancer. And then she had a stroke that took away her ability to communicate with anyone, which made it necessary for her to stay at a nursing home for therapy.

We had just gotten back into each other's lives after years of separation. To have her near me again after so long was a joy, and I did not want it to end so soon in death. Naturally I wanted her to be miraculously healed by God. I know, though, that whenever God has a plan I must sit back and let HIM carry on. In the Bible, for instance, a Shunammite woman's son had just died, yet the woman believed that God's prophet Elishah could still work some kind of miracle to extend his life, which is exactly what happened. Likewise, I wanted to believe to the very end for my daughter's supernatural healing.

Little did I know that my daughter's miracle was to transpire in another way. When Cheri's son David called me to come see his mother for the last time, I knew I was to tell her something.

When I got to the hospital, everyone was out in the hall talking of various things. David quietly said to me, "Go in, Grandma, she's waiting for you."

I went in, sat down and took her hand. Out of my mouth came the words, "I'm jealous of you." Her eyes widened, waiting for some clarification. "You're going to meet our Jesus before I do! And I will try to finish your story of Marie for you."

The Lord gave me a wonderful, calm feeling knowing I would see Cheri again someday. With that amazing hope inside of her, too, Cheri gave up the ghost and died peacefully.

Following that moment, I was now on my own mission to tell the story of Marie Michell Robinson, maybe the youngest WASP who had graduated from training school, and of my daughter Cheri's incredible efforts to do all she could to ensure Marie received the honors she deserved. Both women accomplished noteworthy things in their life on earth and serve as bright examples of what we can achieve through dedication and hard work. Their faith in God is an inspiration for all generations.

Cheri died on May 18, 2016. She was buried on May 23rd, which also happens to be Marie's birthday. At Cheri's funeral, an audio recording of her own voice reading "Celestial Flight" was played for the eulogy. You can hear this recording with accompanying video on YouTube. Search for "Celestial Flight – The Song" on the website. Some of the video was shot with Cheri flying in a B-25 from the Tico Warbird Museum in Titusville, FL, to MacDill AFB in Tampa, FL, where she represented the WASPs in a military exhibit in March 2010.

Another website you will enjoy is www.38wasp.blogspot.com, which Cheri created and developed to honor the WASPs and their families.

Portrait of Marie Michell Robinson, who died at the age of 20 years, 4 months and 10 days, having served as a soaring pioneer in her brief lifetime

ABOUT THE AUTHOR

Therese Marie Clawson was born in Royal Oak, Michigan, growing up right across from The National Shrine of the Little Flower where Father Charles E. Coughlin, the famous radio priest of the 1930s, served as pastor for four decades. Her father, H. Lloyd Clawson, was mayor or commissioner of the city for about 24 years, as well as a realtor who donated the property for Fr. Coughlin's original church. Her parents, siblings and childhood friends all called her "T.C."

T.C. married Roy Michell, the brother of Marie Michell Robinson. Marie had died prior to their marriage, however, so T.C. never had the opportunity to do the usual sister-in-law activities with Marie. T.C.'s and Roy's daughter, Cheryl Marie Michell, is the niece who worked hard to make sure her aunt was properly honored for her achievements as a WASP.

T.C.'s life accomplishments are quite noteworthy. She attended Highland Park Jr. College, Florida Southern College, the University of Michigan and Wayne State University, at which point her family called her a perpetual student. After marrying and having four children, she finally graduated from Oakland University at the same time her oldest son graduated from high school. She translated those educational achievements into becoming a very successful business owner. Along with her husband, James Christman, she became co-founder and director of the Christman Assisted Living Facility in Royal Oak, Michigan.

T.C. has written two other books: *The Mayor's Daughter: A Royal Oak Trilogy* and *Sweet Adeline*. *The Mayor's Daughter: A Royal Oak Trilogy* delves into her fond memories of her dad, Father Coughlin, and her brother, Lloyd "Bud" Clawson, who died in a tragic plane accident during WWII. *Sweet Adeline* tells the incredible story of T.C.'s grandmother, Adeline Herzog.

In addition to being an author, T.C. is an accomplished artist as well. Much of her artwork has been compiled in the book entitled *Paintings By Therese*.